THE WHIMSY O

THE WHIMSY OF
DANK JU-JU

By Sascha Aurora Akhtar

THE EMMA PRESS

First published in the UK in 2019 by the Emma Press Ltd

Poems copyright © Sascha Aurora Akhtar 2019

All rights reserved.

The right of Sascha Aurora Akhtar to be identified as the
author of this work has been asserted in accordance with the
Copyright, Designs and Patents Act 1988.

Edited by Charlotte Geater
Typeset by Emma Wright

ISBN 978-1-912915-27-9

A CIP catalogue record of this book
is available from the British Library.

Printed and bound in the UK
by Oxuniprint Ltd, Oxford.

The Emma Press
theemmapress.com
hello@theemmapress.com
Birmingham, UK

CONTENTS

Girl Child Of The Eighties

Twisty-furled
Yellow-balled
Put on throat
Clunk-foot me geesy face
Matt plays the drums
I put my necklace on
like Barbie
I sit
pink & delicious

rockstarangelfacebridaldreamglowpeaches&cream
My First   Twirly Curls
I had 'em all
Magic girl
I am 'em all

Butterfly chair
    Pomegranate lair
I is spent
I lose my hair
like crayons in a box
      of crayons
lined up
   each colour, each colour
   I line up

Freeze Fry Fist Dried
First Born Unborn child
   eyes crys eyes crys
   I crack up

  I cat, I bat

Anatomy Of A Car-Crash

what are the skeins of / strains of lie
grafted on the table

what is the tiniest something in your eye
all night & into the next day

a searing vestibule
& you are listening
hold it right there taxonomy

there are jumper cables for the erudite
& less engaged of space

a perpetual sniffling
sitting next to the Sikh at the bus-stop

Shibuki avenger
crumple my walls
hold a carnival in my wake

one man's jaw drop is another's
flagrant ember clasp

pry ring finger pray pyre of glass peas
fell from his pocket

& covered the highway stretched
as far as the open mind

rides again a parsnip
a junket river of celery glass
river ribbons

inscribe it song, be bones
like grit true.

Nocturnal Emissions

My tum-e is nuts & bolts
My nightshift is armour
I find myself beleaguered
by inquisitive words
Nestling in yakking
notebooks with sultry lines
It is still I, I find
Craving the lucidity of sleep

haunted by mornings of waking dreams

I grasp nothing by its light
this day temporal module
Only obsession, compulsion
I fear it is for hate

Whilst the nocturne is, is for love

Line

submit   alley
        heat   shock
flash   crack
        sickofdreams
submit   journey
              a   x   i   s
malaise   antiquity
        doubt   play
                    of swan
                    on swan
                    on swan
                    on swan

The Moon On Wednesday

I

the brown & red
the black & blue
hurts me when I hear / see

a measurefold
singing angular
I hold my knees
smiling at the sun
coming in through the leaves
in the rain park

journey me on, on
it rides as a fisher-king does
in the back dark.

I saw the moon on Wednesday
I was beside myself in twos
listening carefully to the man in tattoos
there are reasons *you know yourself now*

you know.

II

I was beside myself
surmise this ~ that trees in winter
have sharper tonguepetals

                              to lick the sky with

The grassblades poke tiny holes
in balloon people, rising

We are funny shapes, us
We hold onto each other's parts, us
melting in summer
plastic puddles of rubberglass

Colours survive, only

if we let them.

III

I see the sidewalk
glistening like a dream in *banarsi*

a naked man entwined with a lamppost,
whispering 'picture' in Italian

Jesus in his skin
Allah in his eyes
Jah on his lips
Gautam in his heart
Shiva in his spine

& Nothing on his mind.

Matutinal

Trying to catch the days of fire burning
      A chrysalis of expectancy, I pupate
      Tri-coloured amorous wings budding
New roses, I have become the secret garden
      Of angel kisses where baby moons
      Sparkle like morello cherries in cloud trees
Each leaf a silky white ribbon
      Waiting to dapple the blue of the sky-dome.

Highway Plein Air I

headlights like,

>>> like *nymphorbs*
>>> if it was the sea

>> it would be glowing
>>> & I would be blind

>>> a seal
>>> in a sky

>>>> cataract
>>>> bowl

>>> each engine rush
>>> a wave
> & I the bobbing buoy
> stare hungrily
> at warm restaurant window
> sitting neatly in a square
> divided by power lines

> moon, fine sharp
> biscuit I am
> a little blood

hanging with twinkling bullet holes
emblazoned

steeple rises
to touch,
but finds it cannot.

I Miss You

When the moonlight decries
its advance guard

the Neu excites
sewing up our two boats
going down
        adjoined in a storm.

I miss you
when abroad in the wintertime squalls

gentle minds alight

                revisioning sleep

a language of queries.

My wish burns bright
as the Neu

as dead on, as delicious

as a psychogeography

                of meeting

at the right moment, over & over.

In Between Days

The restless in I, nods
to the reckless in I, tripping
over my halves, faster
now new moon turns to bacon
in full view, a hooded girl inspects the sky
where we are watching
    Being transported

When lovely, the sunset
could be the eye of an *ism*,
when madness turns
to lovely, I'll be there
obliterated

On arrival, the uncanny sensation
of seeing the thick pile carpet of city
spread out like one's own brain
& you are walking on it
On departure, behind a counter
a woman reminds me of the absence of angels;
the reckoning eldritch seem closer
than last night, the last night,
in dance & paranoia
& belly shoe moves

& wasted

& wasted, nice was
evol, a tune in the current
other minds felt presence, mine
in utero is marching, was you said
Metamorphosis.

On the bank of the thames, t.s. & I see
the bridge rise & fall
to allow the passing of a relic,
& clockwork commands many more
astute ways to wander simultaneous
each bodily function shows you are in overdrive

Unbalanced, hold your shoulder colder
I am drunken over the Atlantic
I don't know where I am
would you give me a flower
& I do not know what time it is
except where I was, always

The Universal Mystique Of Not-Writing

I am not a stylish hand
You are not red clover tea
I am a basker waiting for sharks
to tread the water in fin-love
& remedy is not vanilla-flavoured
orange tetrahedron or gargoyles
pretending to be pretty.

I am not a leather rose
You are not a leaping lemon
There is a memory that has blistered
into letters on my face
I have not held a baby
There is a repose in silence
Joining hands we become
a chain of paper dolls
rippling like hair caught in the current.

I am not a Chinese ant
You are not a velvet molar
A feather-edge
A carbuncle
A season
I tread crushed ice-cubes
There is no other side.

You tie yourself to me
We jump in a pond
hoping to drown
& come up with lily pads in our mouths
Slimy bodies embracing rhetoric.

All I Want Is

intangible, sometimes magnetic
often mesmerising like a field
of buttons, creamy & illuminate
like butter, melting in a bowl
of white porcelain.

All I want is
livid, sometimes violent
always tremendous like a skyscraper
pointing towards the evenstar
coruscating like the teeth of sharks
in movies where people crash into the sea.

All I want is
soft-spoken, edible like houses
made of the bread of ginger, woven
intricate & neat depicting hybrid
fantastical creatures & rugged vines
like the ancient Persian carpet in my grandmother's living room.

All I want is
a poem that sings
of melodious tings.

Maya

small
sugar ladies
& pretzels give
me fervour & boundless
energy to recover from eggy
indiscretions in the hope that I will
knock twice & find once the merryweather
flock of night-time seagulls that timidly arrange
themselves by flight of another crayon, smoking on
the hour forgives me not a saline edge to my bed of gourds
bumping into the walls of a pledge made without any notion to
uncover the next phase of letters written in harmony for fun & Fiction
rings so loud it hears itself on the next continent removed from all sorts of
textual visibility shot through like silk alabaster tissue fields dancing with
paper trails to follow into holes in skin hills & mouldy
orange groves competing for space
with leather lemon trees & lucky charm wells caving
in at the mouth of the hand like ringworms in wooden floors polished to
perfection with oil-soap & sweat beads strung into a harpsichord at odds with
the levitational
skill of monkeys & thieves preparing for a night at the theatre
skill of monkeys & thieves preparing for a night at the theatre
of swords & rude sunbeams wait for silly fish to give up
their belongings & function as active citizens in this
great state of dysphonia an allusion to the shock
of outer shells in learning the flesh within
has no brain or disorder with which
to muse & perpetuate effective
credo for lonely chefs with
bunions to get to the
other side &
wait. 14

Universe

Curl up to one thousand
& one note higher
the next is not
announced, I find you
sharp & sweet
like numerics
& lose yourself
in me there is another
plain bass locked
surrounding like drowning
there is no end to the words I play

like pilfered pockets.

With The Faery

Buttercream-yellow walls of rain
whistling like flowers

Heather wings hang on silken threads
falling as a rope ladder to the moon

Drifting amidst the ocular cloud-
towers, arms tower, head is a large glass bulb

Planted in the rooftop of the world is
where we dance a mélange of song-boats &

aquamarine, wiser for lakes of folklore
unfold secret microcosms of universe.

I pare apples & dangle the peels in my hair,
romantic notions of howling wildebeests

shining in Swedish ultra-sway night,
remembered because of which I am.

Who is hearing wild dogs
barking, it enters me

& if we followed you all night
we'd arrive at day.

Untitled

Sleep is a slowing down
mnemonic to straddle as your cheeks
blow outwards rapidly like shirt cuffs
on the washing-line whilst the fingers
hold the pen of steel, gripping
your night closely

Dead fathers & lost angels
fly above your head as you search
for enigmatic smiles on faces
carved out of jade in the chasms
of blisskarma which tastes
like anything but

When you dive headlong
into summer sheets soaked
with sebum & semen, you grow
like a windfire which courts you, your senses, your apathy
your energy, your empress neck
has torn & silent reeds
flourish in the zero circle
inside your grace
& amplitude; the multiple waves
roll over each other washing
your face away to drift
cooing at the pelicans

as they snatch your eyes
from the ocean visage, crying.

I recognise only them.

Chronotope

ta panta rhei

alabaster has a naming
picture, frozen

there is no difference
between sky & stone-to-stone

raw welt, imagined

feet rubbed with leaves
sapphire disco, decision

stiletto still voice
bevel-headed learning

time-font consideration

secede close circumcision
recall no end, heaven
lie list lip
cerebrum, cerebellum evince

spark

fast rolling water, move.

Chaos Totem

If it is,
      condors in the night sky
a gilded wooing eruption
in the empress way of stars,
I hear each bar of the xylophone
beaten by their wings
battling the atmosphere.

A wish to pass
behind the firewall, you.

If it is,
      fire-starters in the dim
in the cavernous, in the ruins of the day
a pacing, piercing undulation
rippling under the skin,
I feel each dig of the claws
of the panther puncturing my lungs
to a paler, slivered shadow of breath.

Your smile glowing
in the tint of a nuclear sun; the dream of red letters
every night, new.

If it is,
      angels of mercy
unfurling ragged wings on runny skies,
I see Sophia's paintings dripping
on my head & each prayer wheel
spins in the temples of Kathmandu
furiously, yellow-bellied pigeons

fall over from lack of oxygen,
eggs are fried on the bonnets of cars
& I hear the Noctiluca
roaring of its hunger.

If it is,
       I draw the line.
I choke the hold on time
& supply runs short.

Shoals of unborns playing tantras with wooden legs
on tankers carrying oil explode
& melt the very tarsoul of the road & you
you must run for your very, very life.

Aethyrs

RESTORATION OF TEMPERATURE

Magnets collide, poles pushing
each other apart, each half
of the brain doing the same, crashing
the front of a car, red, burning
into a wall rhythmic & repeated

Ramming into the bricks, bleeding
at the joints, the car is redder now,
my medulla love oblongata tending
the sails aloft & blossoming outwards
in a kiss-filled driving wind; Will, shining
phallus of a female reading portents
in the moonscape of a cloudy night

Rising like death in a gas chamber,
ambles with six legs of an arachnid, the carver
of slumber into nightmarish waltzes with familials

Jaws yawning & you
reflected in the epiglottis
hanging in the cavern of the throat
where words ring pealing like awakenings.

Under this heat-maddened sky
of language & commerce, donkeys rot
next to pye-dogs that rule
the streets of days & night
howling into forms that manifest
suspended above our beds like rain

frozen in a pause

a blink; each moment flows
in a circuitous emblem
designed to signify this immersion of senses,
a vice grip keeping the head down; breath
is all you can take, the mercury falling,
your abdomen a lilting cadence

the beginning song rustling through imaginary leaves
on trees festooned with glowing cups
ripe swords, sun-kissed wands

& lush pentacles.

THE ALCHEMIST'S FORMULA

I sour mavens
& invent precision
A cut-glass time lozenge
lies sparking, inviting fingers to turn
Your marble gaze is opening doors
Creatures spasm like hot rocks
in your oral cavity.

Beckon to Aten
Roll a naming up like tobacco leaf
Even animals dream, my dreams.

On pointed twists of tele-paper
I prompt you
to find the nautilus.

Leave the veil for the morning
& suppose the gentle beheads itself

or torture on purpose
or Samoan juggernauts
or pink shocking
or cod-piece, my mouthpiece.

Eat 4x4x4 rock-candy cages
sizzle of you
like die, crest
up against a body
baked in pepper
I encrust you.

Sails slap against your face
I harpoon an ant
I send juniper berries to the sun
Collapse like an exhausted dulcet
& brown tubers lightly

like sea-salt sprinkled on a snail.

The Muse Bewilders

This evening is a violent riot
of technicolour eyes living
vicarious in 'I' lives, in you

whose sun has traversed its arc of sky,

whose afternoon shadows pale in the window.

A winter in effect glistening, remote
& I hear ears throbbing,
the radiation you gave me

a lost beginning

a shoulder blade to cry on

a glowing foetus.

My many hours collide invisibly
& you tend them like breath-flowers
to press in your pages of mirth.
If I taste you, temptress,
my spinal cord pricks, wings shoot
through my back like wind blowing
through whistles, like a friend
haunting me. Icicles hang over my trachea
when I am spoken to, I bark
like a salamander, I pass out
like a light switch.

I embezzle you
crooked as a storm in blazing hay
when you picture, hear diamonds
invent riddles in a can of worms.

When you were a movement, I positioned it
casting beeswax candles of your face,
I throw pots the shape of your sacrum
& kiss the coccyx

hardening like my arteries.

ACKNOWLEDGEMENTS

'The Stranger' was first published in *Only Dying Sparkles* (ZimZalla Press, 2018), a poetic and visual sequence in the form of a tarot-inspired card deck, which was a collaboration between Sascha and the artist John Alexander Arnold

'The Muse Bewilders', 'Chaos Totem', 'Anatomy Of A Car-Crash', 'The Universal Mystique Of Not-Writing' and 'The Alchemist's Formula' have all been published on the Poetry International Rotterdam Website.

'Girl Child Of The Eighties' first appeared in the anthology *Catechism: Poems For Pussy Riot*, published by English PEN in 2013.

ABOUT THE POET

Sascha Aurora Akhtar feels deeply connected to her ancestral roots in Lancashire, South Yorkshire and Pakistan. Born into a literary family, with writers of both fiction and poetry represented, Sascha has been naturally drawn towards many kinds of writing.

Her first poetry collection was *The Grimoire of Grimalkin* (Salt, 2007), followed by *199 Japanese Names for Japanese Trees* (Shearsman, 2016) and *Only Dying Sparkles* (zimZalla, 2018). Her fiction has appeared in *BlazeVox, Tears In The Fence, The Learned Pig, Anti-Heroin Chic* and *Storgy*. Sascha has performed internationally at festivals such as the Poetry International Festival in Rotterdam, Avantgarde Festival in Hamburg, and Southbank Centre's Meltdown festival in London, curated by Yoko Ono.

ABOUT THE EMMA PRESS

The Emma Press is an independent publisher dedicated to producing beautiful, thought-provoking books. It was founded in 2012 by Emma Dai'an Wright in Winnersh, UK, and is now based in the Jewellery Quarter, Birmingham.

The Emma Press publishes poetry and fiction anthologies and pamphlets for adults and for children, with a growing list of translations.

The Emma Press has been shortlisted for the Michael Marks Award for Poetry Pamphlet Publishers in 2014, 2015, 2016 and 2018, winning in 2016.

theemmapress.com
emmavalleypress.blogspot.co.uk